SO·ON·EARTH

To Sylvia.
   From Janis April 2001. xx.

A·LITTLE·BOOK·OF INSPIRATION

A·LITTLE·BOOK OF·INSPIRATION

CICELY MARY BARKER

◆

FREDERICK WARNE

The reproductions in this book have been made using the most modern electronic scanning methods from entirely new transparencies of Cicely Mary Barker's original watercolours. They enable Cicely Mary Barker's skill as an artist to be appreciated as never before.

FREDERICK WARNE
Published by the Penguin Group
Penguin Books Ltd, 27 Wrights Lane, London W8 5TZ, England
Penguin Putnam Inc., 375 Hudson Street, New York, N.Y. 10014, USA
Penguin Books Australia Ltd, Ringwood, Victoria, Australia
Penguin Books Canada Ltd, 10 Alcorn Avenue, Toronto, Ontario, Canada M4V 3B2
Penguin Books (N.Z.) Ltd, Private Bag 102902, NSMC, Auckland

Penguin Books Ltd, Registered Offices: Harmondsworth, Middlesex, England

First published 2000

1 3 5 7 9 10 8 6 4 2

ISBN 0 7232 4597 5

Colour reproduction by Saxon
Printed and bound in Great Britain by
William Clowes Limited, Beccles and London

Shine upon me, Lord
and I shall be light like the day.

ORTHODOX PRAYER

◆

The people that walked in darkness
have seen a great light: they that dwell
in the land of the shadow of death,
upon them hath the light shined.

ISAIAH 9, 2

◆

I found him nearest when I missed him most;
I found him in my heart, a life in frost,
A light I knew not till my soul was dark.

GEORGE MACDONALD, *Lost and Found*

Our life is a long and arduous
quest after Truth.

MAHATMA GHANDI

the leaves believe
such letting go is love
such love is faith
such faith is grace
such grace is God.
I agree with the leaves.

LUCILLE CLIFTON

Today is the tomorrow you
worried about yesterday.

ANON

I give you the end of a golden string;
Only wind it into a ball,
It will lead you in at Heaven's gate,
Built in Jerusalem's wall.

WILLIAM BLAKE

◆

Better to light a candle than
to curse the darkness.

CHINESE PROVERB

◆

Henceforth let your souls alway
Make each morn an Easter Day.

GERARD MANLEY HOPKINS, *Easter*

I looked at the sea
And on further to the high stars.
The whole world was full of wonders . . .
It seemed all one great miracle
Ranged too wide for me to record.

WILLIAM LANGLAND, *Piers Plowman*
(translated by Ronald Tamplin)

To see a World in a Grain of Sand
And a Heaven in a Wild Flower,
Hold Infinity in the palm of your hand
And Eternity in an hour.

WILLIAM BLAKE, *Auguries of Innocence*

All things bright and beautiful,
All creatures great and small,
All things wise and wonderful,
The Lord God made them all.

C. F. ALEXANDER

God never wrought miracle to
convince atheism, because his
ordinary works convince it.

FRANCIS BACON

Dear Father
hear and bless
Thy beasts and singing birds;
And guard
with tenderness
small things
that have no words.

ANON

It is only with the Heart that
one can see rightly;
What is essential is invisible
to the eye.

ANTOINE DE SAINTE-EXUPERY

I share creation,
Kings can do no more.

ANON, CHINESE

Salvation dwells with the Lord,
With Christ, the Omnipotent Word.
From generation to generation
Grant us, O Lord, Thy grace and salvation!

JAMES CLARENCE MANGAN,
St Patrick's Hymn Before Tara (from the Irish)

Through all Eternity to Thee
A joyful Song I'll raise,
For oh! Eternity's too short
To utter all thy Praise.

JOSEPH ADDISON

No coward soul is mine,
No trembler in the world's
storm-troubled sphere:
I see Heaven's glories shine,
And faith shines equal,
arming me from fear.

EMILY BRONTË, *Last Lines*

Little deeds of kindness,
Little words of love,
Help to make earth happy,
Like the heavens above.

JULIA CARNEY

Character cannot be developed in ease and quiet. Only through experience of trial and suffering can the soul be strengthened, ambition inspired, and success achieved.

HELEN KELLER

Three things are necessary for the salvation of man: to know what he ought to believe; to know what he ought to desire; and to know what he ought to do.

THOMAS AQUINAS

Never let anything so fill you with sorrow as to make you forget the joy of the Christ risen.

MOTHER TERESA

Matthew, Mark, Luke, and John,
Bless the bed that I lie on.
Four corners to my bed,
Four Angels there be spread:
One at the head, one at the feet,
And two to guard me while I sleep.
God within, and God without,
And Jesus Christ all round about;
If any danger come to me,
Sweet Jesus Christ deliver me.

ANON

Close now thine eyes, and rest secure;
Thy soul is safe enough, thy body sure;
He that loves thee, he that keeps
And guards thee, never slumbers, never sleeps . . .

FRANCIS QUARLES, *A Good-Night*

From Ghosties and Ghoulies
And long-leggity Beasties,
And all things that go BUMP
in the night –
Good Lord, deliver us!

ANON

God bless the inventor of sleep, the cloak
that covers all men's thoughts, the food
that cures all hunger . . . the balancing
weight that levels the shepherd with the
king and the simple with the wise.

MIGUEL CERVANTES, *Don Quixote*

Now I lay me down to sleep
I pray that Christ my soul will keep;
If I should die before I wake,
I pray that Christ my soul will take.

ANON

Suffer the little children to come unto me,
and forbid them not; for of such is
the kingdom of God. Verily I say
unto you, Whosoever shall not receive
the kingdom of God as a little child,
he shall not enter therein.

MARK 10, 14-15

To live is not to live for one's self alone;
let us help one another.

MENANDER

So let us love, deare Love, like as we ought,
– Love is the lesson which the Lord us taught.

EDMUND SPENSER, *Easter Sunday*

Have you had a kindness shown?
Pass it on;
'Twas not given for thee alone,
Pass it on;
Let it travel down the years,
Let it wipe another's tears,
Till in heaven the deed appears –
Pass it on.

HENRY BURTON

Even if happiness forgets you a little bit,
never completely forget about it.

JACQUES PREVERT

28

He who binds to himself a joy
Does the winged life destroy;
But he who kisses the joy as it flies
Lives in Eternity's sunrise.

WILLIAM BLAKE, *Joy*

God is a circle whose centre is everywhere
and whose circumference is nowhere.

EMPEDOCLES

Ah, but a man's reach should exceed his
grasp, or what's a heaven for?

ROBERT BROWNING

Make us worthy, Lord,
To serve our fellow-men
Throughout the world who live and die
In poverty or hunger.
Give them, through our hands
This day their daily bread,
And by our understanding love,
Give peace and joy.

MOTHER TERESA

The reaping men and women paused
And sat down where they stood;
They ate and drank and were refreshed,
For rest from toil is good.

CHRISTINA ROSSETTI, *In a Cornfield*

And all shall be well and all shall be well,
and all manner of things shall be well.

JULIANA OF NORWICH, *Revelations of Divine Love*

Live as if to die tomorrow
Learn as if to live forever.

MAHATMA GHANDI

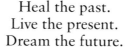

Heal the past.
Live the present.
Dream the future.

ANON

The voyage of discovery lies not in finding
new landscapes,
But in having new eyes.

MARCEL PROUST

Doubt sees the obstacles
Faith sees the way.
Doubt sees the darkest night
Faith sees the day.
Doubt dreads to take a step
Faith soars on high.
Doubt questions, 'Who believes?'
Faith answers, 'I.'

ANON

God be in my head,
And in my understanding;

God be in mine eyes,
And in my looking;

God be in my mouth,
And in my speaking;

God be in my heart,
and in my thinking;

God be at my end,
And at my departing.

ANON

Deep peace of the Running Wave to you.
Deep peace of the Flowing Air to you.
Deep peace of the Quiet Earth to you.
Deep peace of the Shining Stars to you.
Deep peace of the Son of Peace to you.

GAELIC BLESSING

Happy the man, and happy he alone,
He who can call today his own;
He who, secure within, can say,
Tomorrow, do thy worst,
for I have lived today!

JOHN DRYDEN, *Translation of Horace, Bk III. xxix*

We are shaped by our thoughts;
we become what we think.
When the mind is pure,
joy follows like a shadow and never leaves.

BUDDHA

Happiness exists not in the multitude of friends but in the worth and choice.

BEN JONSON

◆

I believe that every right implies a responsibility; every opportunity an obligation; every possession a duty.

JOHN D. ROCKEFELLER

What God gives, and what we take,
'Tis a gift for Christ His sake;
Be the meal of Beans and Pease
God be thanked for those, and these:
Have we flesh, or have we fish,
All are fragments from His dish.

ANON

Pray we to God, the Almighty Lord,
That sendeth food to beasts and men,
To send His blessing on this board,
To feed us now and ever, Amen.

ANON

I see the moon,
And the moon sees me;
God bless the moon,
And God bless me.

ANON

God loves a cheerful giver;
she gives most who gives with joy.

MOTHER TERESA

The rain it raineth on the just,
And also on the unjust fella,
But chiefly on the just, because
The unjust steals the just's umbrella.

CHARLES, BARON BOWEN

Nothing in life is to be feared.
It is only to be understood.

MARIE CURIE

◆

I do not feel obliged to believe that the
same God who has endowed us with sense,
reason and intellect intended us to forgo
their use.

GALILEO GALILEI

◆

Time is a companion that goes with us on
a journey. It reminds us to cherish each
moment, because it will never come again.
What we leave behind is not as important
as how we have lived.

PATRICK STEWART

He that is down needs fear no fall,
He that is low, no pride;
He that is humble ever shall
Have God to be his guide.

JOHN BUNYAN

This is my simple religion.
There is no need for temples;
no need for complicated philosophy.
Our own heart is the temple;
the philosophy is kindness.

DALAI LAMA

To give pleasure to a single heart
by a single kind act is better than
a thousand head-bowings in prayer.

SADDI

Religion is a candle inside a multicoloured lantern. Everyone looks through a particular colour, but the candle is always there.

MOHAMMED NEGUIB

Therefore be ye lamps unto yourselves, be a refuge to yourselves. Hold fast to Truth as a lamp; hold fast to Truth as a refuge. Look not for a refuge in anyone beside yourselves. And those, who shall be a lamp unto themselves betake themselves to no external refuge, but holding fast to the Truth as their lamp, and holding fast to the Truth as their refuge, they shall reach the topmost height.

BUDDHA

Real knowledge is to know the extent of one's ignorance.

CONFUCIUS

Expecting Him, my door was open wide:
Then I looked round
If any lack of service might be found,
And saw Him at my side:
How entered, by what secret stair,
I know not, knowing only He was there.

T. E. BROWN, *Presence*

O Divine Master, grant that
I may not so much seek
to be consoled as to console;
to be understood as to understand;
to be loved, as to love;
for it is in giving that we receive,
it is in pardoning that we are pardoned,
and it is in dying that we are born
to eternal life.

St. Francis of Assisi

God grant me
the serenity to
accept the things
I cannot change,
courage to change
the things I can,
and wisdom
to know the
difference.

ANON

Science without Religion is lame.
Religion without Science is blind.

ALBERT EINSTEIN

Life is itself but the shadow of death,
and souls departed but the shadows of
the living. All things fall under this name.
The sun itself is but the dark simulacrum,
and light but the shadow of God.

SIR THOMAS BROWNE

I saw Eternity the other night
Like a great Ring of pure and endless light,
All calm, as it was bright;
And round beneath it,
Time in hours, days, years,
Driven by the spheres
Like a vast shadow moved, in which the world
And all her train were hurled.

HENRY VAUGHAN, *The World*

The Lord is my shepherd; I shall not want.
He maketh me to lie down in green pastures:
He leadeth me beside the still waters.
He restoreth my soul: He leadeth me in the
paths of righteousness for His name's sake.
Yea, though I walk through the valley of the
shadow of death, I will fear no evil:
for thou art with me;
thy rod and thy staff they comfort me.

PSALM 23, 1-4

Who is it who throws light into the meeting
on the mountain?
Who announces the ages of the moon?
Who teaches the place where couches the sun?

ANON

Little flower – but if I could understand
What you are, root and all, all in all,
I should know what God and man is.

ALFRED, LORD TENNYSON,
Flower in the Crannied Wall

It is the quality of our work which will
please God and not the quantity.

MAHATMA GANDHI

◆

All that we ought to have thought
and have not thought,
All that we ought to have said,
and have not said,
All that we ought to have done,
and have not done,
All that we ought not to have thought,
and yet have thought,
All that we ought not to have said,
and yet have said,
All that we ought not to have done,
and yet have done,
For all these words, and deeds, O God,
We pray for forgiveness,
and repent with penance.

ZOROASTER

And so, we have come, Lady,
Our day's work done;
Our love, our hopes, our selves
We give to your son.

CLIVE SANSOM, *The Shepherd's Carol*

What shall I give him,
Poor as I am?
If I were a shepherd,
I would give a lamb.
If I were a wise man,
I would do my part,
Yet, what I can I give him,
Give my heart.

CHRISTINA ROSSETTI, *A Christmas Carol*

And not by eastern windows only,
When daylight comes, comes in the light,
In front the sun climbs slow, how slowly,
But westward, look, the land is bright.

ARTHUR HUGH CLOUGH,
Say Not the Struggle Nought Availeth

'How many miles to Babylon?'
'Three-score and ten.'
'Can I get there by candlelight?'
'Yes, and back again.
If your heels are nimble and light,
You may get there by candle-light.'

ANON

'Bless, O Lord, this day of days.
Bless with riches all our ways.

DAVID ADAM

Goodness, love, grace and gentleness,
Courtesy, friendship and modesty,
Honesty, penance and chastity,
Charity, respect, reverence and truthfulness,
Purity and self-control, wisdom and worship,
All these together are perfect virtue,
And are the word of the loving Lord.

HINDU PRAYER

This is that night – no, day, grown great with bliss,
   In which the power of Satan broken is;
   In heaven be glory, peace unto the earth!

WILLIAM DRUMMOND, *The Angels for the Nativity of Our Lord*

   Christ cannot find a chamber in the inn.
   We entertain Him always like a stranger,
And, as at first, still lodge Him in the manger.

ANON

Dear Father, help me with the love
That casteth out all fear.
Teach me to lean on thee, and feel
That thou art very near;
That no temptation is unseen,
No childish grief too small,
Since thou, with patience infinite,
Dost soothe and comfort all.

LOUISA M. ALCOTT

Show me a thoroughly satisfied man
and I will show you a failure.

THOMAS EDISON

Nothing great was ever achieved
without enthusiasm.

RALPH WALDO EMERSON

Anytime the going seems easy, better check
and see if you are going downhill.

ANON

So shall my walk be close with God,
Calm and serene my frame;
So purer light shall mark the road
That leads me to the Lamb.

WILLIAM COWPER

And God shall wipe away all tears from their eyes; and there shall be no more sorrow, nor crying, neither shall there be any more pain: for the former things are passed away.

REVELATIONS 21, 4

◆

Praise the Lord! ye heavens adore Him,
Praise Him, Angels in the height!

JOHN KEMPTHORNE

◆

Redeem thy mis-spent time that's past;
Live this day as if 'twere thy last.

BISHOP THOMAS KEN

Watch your thoughts; they become words.
Watch your words, they become actions.
Watch your actions, they become habits.
Watch your habits, they become character.
Watch your character, it becomes your destiny.

ANON

Don't go around saying the world
owes you a living; the world owes you nothing;
it was here first.

MARK TWAIN

Success is a matter of luck . . .
ask any failure.

EARL WILSON

Man is the only animal that laughs and
weeps; for he is the only animal that is
struck with the difference between what
things are and what they ought to be.
WILLIAM HAZLITT

Life is a grindstone. Whether it grinds you
down or polishes you up depends on what
you are made of.

ANON

Praised be my Lord for our mother the earth,
who doth sustain and keep us,
And bringest forth divers fruits
and flowers of many colours, and grass.

St Francis of Assisi

All things counter, original, spare, strange;
Whatever is fickle, freckled (who knows how?)
With swift, slow; sweet, sour; adazzle, dim;
He fathers-forth whose beauty is past change.
Praise him.

Gerard Manley Hopkins, *Pied Beauty*

First the seed and then the grain;
Thank you, God, for sun and rain.
First the flour and then the bread;
Thank you, God, that we are fed.
Thank you, God, for all your care;
Help us all to share and share.

TRADITIONAL

The earth does not belong to man;
man belongs to the earth.

CHIEF SEATTLE

Only when the last tree has died
and the last river has been poisoned
and the last fish has been caught
will we realise that we cannot eat money.

AMERICAN INDIAN SAYING

Shoot for the moon. Even if you miss,
you'll land among the stars.

LES BROWN

Yesterday is history;
tomorrow is a mystery.
Today is a gift;
that's why we call it the present.

ANON

He Prayeth best, who loveth best
All things both great and small;
For the dear God who loveth us,
He made and loveth all.

SAMUEL TAYLOR COLERIDGE

You never enjoy the world aright, till the
sea itself gloweth in your veins, till you are
clothed with the heavens and crowned
with the stars; and perceive yourself to be
the sole heir of the world, and more than
so, because men are in it who are every one
sole heirs as well as you.

THOMAS TRAHERNE, *Centuries of Meditations*

Love is like the wild rose-briar;
Friendship like the holly-tree.
The holly is dark when the rose-briar blooms,
But which will bloom most constantly?

EMILY BRONTË

The only reward of virtue is virtue; the only
way to have a friend is to be one.

RALPH WALDO EMERSON

The greatest sweetener of human life is
Friendship. To raise this to the highest
pitch of enjoyment, is a secret which
but few discover.

JOSEPH ADDISON

Fate chooses your relations,
you choose your friends.

JACQUES DELILLE

Old friends are best.
King James used to call for his old shoes;
they were easiest for his feet.

JOHN SELDEN

The eternal God is thy refuge,
and underneath are the everlasting arms.

DEUTERONOMY 33, 27

Death be not proud,
though some have called thee
Mighty and dreadful,
for thou art not so,
For those whom thou think'st
thou dost overthrow
Die not, poor death,
nor yet canst thou kill me . . .
One short sleep past,
we wake eternally,
And death shall be no more;
death, thou shalt die.

JOHN DONNE, *Divine Poems X*

Fear no more the heat o' the sun
Nor the furious winter's rages;
Thou thy worldly task hast done,
Home art gone and ta'en thy wages:
Golden lads and girls all must,
As chimney-sweepers, come to dust.

WILLIAM SHAKESPEARE, *Cymbeline*

Is it so small a thing
To have enjoyed the sun,
To have lived light in the spring,
To have loved, to have thought, to have done;
To have advanced true friends,
And beat down baffling foes?

MATTHEW ARNOLD, *Empedocles on Etna*

And still, O Lord, to me impart
An innocent and grateful heart,
That after my great sleep I may
Awake to thy eternal day! Amen.

SAMUEL TAYLOR COLERIDGE,
A Child's Evening Prayer

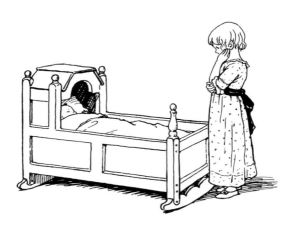